IT'S TRUE!

DINOSAURS NEVER DIED

Other  titles

There Are Bugs in Your Bed
Heather Catchpole & Vanessa Woods   PICTURES BY Craig Smith

Pigs Do Fly
Terry Denton   PICTURES BY Terry Denton

Fashion Can Be Fatal
Susan Green   PICTURES BY Gregory Rogers

Your Hair Grows 15 Kilometres a Year
Diana Lawrenson   PICTURES BY Leigh Hobbs

Crime Doesn't Pay
Beverley MacDonald   CARTOONS BY Andrew Weldon

A Bushfire Burned My Dunny Down
Tracey McGuire   PICTURES BY Bill Wood

We Came From Slime
Ken McNamara   PICTURES BY Andrew Plant

Frogs Are Cannibals
Michael Tyler   PICTURES BY Mic Looby

The Romans Were the Real Gangsters
John & Joshua Wright   PICTURES BY Joshua Wright

JOHN LONG
PICTURES BY TRAVIS TISCHLER

IT'S TRUE!

DINOSAURS NEVER DIED

ALLEN&UNWIN

For Heather, who came to the desert
to dig up fossils and never looked back!

First published in 2004

Allen & Unwin
83 Alexander Street
Crows Nest NSW 2065
Australia
Phone: (61 2) 8425 0100
Fax: (61 2) 9906 2218
Email: info@allenandunwin.com
Web: www.allenandunwin.com

National Library of Australia
Cataloguing-in-Publication entry:

Long, John A. 1957– .
It's true! dinosaurs never died.
For children aged 8–12 years.
ISBN 1 74114 274 1.
1. Dinosaurs – Juvenile literature. I. Tischler, Travis. II. Title.
567.9

Series, cover and text design by Ruth Grüner
Cover photograph: J. Krasemann Stephen/Photolibrary.com
Set in 12.5pt Minion by Ruth Grüner
Printed by McPherson's Printing Group

1 3 5 7 9 10 8 6 4 2

**Teaching notes for the It's True! series are available
on the website: www.itstrue.com.au**

CONTENTS

WHY DINOSAURS?

1

WHAT ON EARTH
ARE DINOSAURS?   viii

Greatest Ever Dinosaur Battles #1

2

HOW DO WE KNOW
ABOUT DINOSAURS?   14

3

MEET THE MEAT-EATERS   24

Greatest Ever Dinosaur Battles #2

4

WORLD'S BIGGEST
(AND DUMBEST?) VEGETARIANS   36

5

WEAPONS OF DESTRUCTION AND DEFENCE:
HORNS AND ARMOUR   44

6

A BUNCH OF WEIRD WEED-MUNCHERS   50

Greatest Ever Dinosaur Battles #3

7

DINOSAUR RUSTLERS AND SMUGGLERS   58

8

INSIDE DINOSAUR DAILY LIVES   64

9

DINOSAURS TAKE TO THE AIR   70

10

DOWNFALL OF THE DINOSAURS   76

Pronunciation guide   83

Thanks   85

Where to find out more   86

Index   87

WHY DINOSAURS?

I started collecting fossils when I was seven, and I've been doing it ever since. In fact, it's now my job – I work at a museum, and my specialty is prehistoric animals, including fossil fish and dinosaurs.

We're constantly finding new dinosaur bones (and sometimes skin or poo or even feathers) that tell us more about these extraordinary beasts – how they fought each other, how they looked after their babies, how far they travelled, how they changed over time, and much more. These dinosaur fossils are in big demand, and are sometimes smuggled overseas and sold illegally. (I once travelled around the world trying to catch a thief who had stolen some dinosaur footprints. It's true!)

So let's go back 150 million years, to the fantastic world of the dinosaurs.

1

WHAT ON EARTH ARE DINOSAURS?

Most of us wouldn't know a real dinosaur if it jumped up and bit us on the bum! It's true! (Mind you, if *T. rex* bit us on the bum, it wouldn't matter.) Everyone thinks that dinosaurs were big scary reptiles that lived millions of years ago in steamy tropical swamps. That's only part of the truth. I've also heard some people refer to crocodiles as 'living dinosaurs'. That's definitely not correct. So let's start by sorting out what you know about dinosaurs.

QUIZ

WHICH OF THESE STATEMENTS ARE CORRECT?

Dinosaurs were reptiles.

True ☐   False ☐

Dinosaurs were warm-blooded.

True ☐   False ☐

Dinosaurs were closely related to crocodiles and snakes.

True ☐   False ☐

Dinosaurs were closely related to birds.

True ☐   False ☐

All dinosaurs died out 65 million years ago, when a meteorite hit Earth.

True ☐   False ☐

All dinosaurs were big and scary.

True ☐   False ☐

Dinosaurs lived in hot, humid climates.

True ☐   False ☐

(answers on page 82)

Dinosaurs were a kind of
reptile, even though they
were probably warm-blooded.
But they were quite different
from other ancient reptiles,
such as crocodiles and alligators.
Crocodilians are the ancestors
of dinosaurs,
but they
aren't dinosaurs.
So what's the difference? The answer lies
not in their massive size, but in their legs and feet.

If you take a close look at a typical lizard or a
crocodile (either on screen or in real life), you'll see that
its arms and legs stick out from the side
of its body. These critters crawl with a
sprawl. Dinosaurs had a totally different
way of moving. Their legs carried their
weight straight down to their toes.
And here's the really interesting
thing: birds also
do this.

2

All birds evolved from a group of upright, walking, meat-eating dinosaurs, and so birds have exactly the same kind of foot structure as a dinosaur.

WHERE DID THE FIRST DINOSAURS COME FROM?

The first dinosaurs evolved from crocodile-like ancestors called 'thecodonts'. These were reptiles that walked on all fours but had a more specialised kind of ankle joint than other reptiles. Think of it like a GTX racing model of the standard ankle. The new improved foot structure helped them to walk upright. Even better, it enabled them to run faster than any other land creature! They were the best at hunting down prey, or running away from danger. This is the main reason why dinosaurs dominated life on Earth for the next 150 million years.

WHAT DOES 'EVOLVED' MEAN?

To evolve means to change over long periods
of time, maybe thousands or millions of years.
Individual animals differ from each other, and some
are better at surviving, so they get to have babies.
Often it's the fastest or the strongest or the ones
with the best beak or teeth or wings or the thickest
fur who survive. Gradually more and more of the
animals of this kind become faster, stronger or
better equipped for a certain climate or situation.
This process of change explains how the first fishes
acquired arms, legs and lungs and were then able
to live on land as air-breathing amphibians.
Eventually there were some amphibians that could
lay hard-shelled eggs – we call them reptiles.
Next came primitive turtles, crocodiles
and dinosaurs.

Evolution happened among the
dinosaurs too. For example, small, beaked
Psittacosaurus evolved into the larger, frilled
Protoceratops, which evolved into the much
larger horned *Triceratops*.

WHEN DID WE FIRST FIND OUT ABOUT DINOSAURS?

Dinosaurs (meaning 'terrible lizard') were first named in 1841 by the English scientist Richard Owen.
His study of fossil bones revealed that the animals they came from walked upright and were not just another group of slow-moving reptiles.

WHERE DID THEY LIVE?
WALKING THE WORLD

We have dug up remains of dinosaurs in every corner of the Earth. Their fossils – the bones, footprints, eggs and nests – have been found in Australia, North America, South America, Europe and Asia, and even in Antarctica.

This tells us something else that's important. Dinosaurs were probably not good swimmers, so they must have walked from one continent to another. This suggests that the continents then were much closer together than they are today.

WHEN DID DINOSAURS LIVE?

Dinosaurs lived in the Mesozoic Era from 250 to 65 million years ago. The Mesozoic Era has been divided into three parts – the Triassic, Jurassic and Cretaceous periods. The first dinosaurs appeared on the Earth around 225 million years ago, in the middle of the Triassic Period. The first furry mammals also appeared at this time, and so did the flying reptiles (called pterosaurs, close cousins of the dinosaurs).

Let's compare these times with the seconds in an hour. There are 3600 seconds in each hour – that's about one second for each million years that life has existed on Earth.

The dinosaurs appear only 3 minutes and 15 seconds before our hour is up. Most of them died out 65 million years ago, equivalent to a minute before the hour. Using the same scale, modern humans appear on the planet less than a second before the hour strikes!

LIFE ON EARTH

The Earth is very, very old – about
4 500 000 000 years old (that's 4.5 billion years).
The main stages of life on Earth are:

3.5 BILLION YEARS AGO
▶ bacteria and algae first appear

540 MYA*
▶ trilobites, shells, corals and other sea life

500 MYA
▶ the first fishes

350 MYA
▶ the first amphibians on land

320 MYA
▶ the first reptiles

225 MYA
▶ the first dinosaurs, pterosaurs and mammals

150 MYA
▶ the first birds

The Mesozoic Era spans 195 million years:

THE TRIASSIC PERIOD ▶ 245–208 MYA

THE JURASSIC PERIOD ▶ 208–145 MYA

THE CRETACEOUS PERIOD ▶ 145–65 MYA

*MYA = million years ago

HOW MANY DINOSAURS?

Every kid can name at least six different dinosaurs. Old favourites are *Tyrannosaurus*, *Triceratops*, *Allosaurus*, *Brachiosaurus*, *Stegosaurus* and *Velociraptor*. But how many more were there?

Over 800 species of dinosaur have been named, but we have complete skeletons for very few of them. There may be only 250 different species in fact. Most of them are known from only a handful of bones, or even one bone or tooth!

DINOSAUR FAMILIES

Scientists have divided dinosaurs into two main kinds:
saurischians and ornithischians. Within each of these
groups are many sub-groups or families. Think of
it like a dinosaur fashion parade or car rally. Each
different model is well suited to a particular lifestyle.

➤ **The lizard-hipped group, or saurischians**

This includes theropods, which are mostly
meat-eaters, and the giant, long-necked
plant-eaters, called sauropods. We'll look at theropods
in chapter 3 and sauropods in chapter 4.

➤ **The bird-hipped group, or ornithischians**

This includes the armoured dinosaurs,
such as *ankylosaurus* and *stegosaurus*, and the horned
dinosaurs or ceratopsians. We'll look at them in chapter 5.
The upright, walking plant-eaters like *Iguanodon* and the
hadrosaurs or duck-billed dinosaurs are also bird-hipped.
You can find out about them in chapter 6.

Oddly, it was some of the lizard-hipped ones that
survived and evolved into birds. There's more about
that in chapter 9.

Greatest Ever Dinosaur Battles #1

Velociraptor v Protoceratops

The *Velociraptor* was wandering alone, away from his pack, not sure of what he might find in this new territory. He was lost, and very hungry. He sniffed the air. Surely that was the smell of a *Protoceratops*? Mmm!

He watched it lumbering along on all fours towards the glade – probably looking for its own lunch of juicy plants. Hiding behind a lone twisted pine, the *Velociraptor* waited for the right moment. Suddenly he leapt, razor-sharp sickle claws ready to strike, and fell on the back of the *Protoceratops* before it had any time to twist away. The huge beast was surprisingly quick to react, thrashing around until it threw the *Velociraptor* to the ground. Then it charged, thrusting forward savagely with its sharpened nose-cone and butting with its heavy head shield. The *Velociraptor* tried biting its face, only to break a tooth on the horny shield.

With just a few seconds free of its enemy, the *Protoceratops* then began to dig itself down into the sand. At the same time, it covered its neck with the head shield, bundling itself up to make an impenetrable fortress.

The *Velociraptor* crouched down to prepare for its last deadly attack. Just then, a huge sandstorm blew in like a wall of doom. It buried them both under a tonne of fine red sand. Both dinosaurs died instantly, crushed by the weight, locked in everlasting battle.

The story you've just read is a true story. I've made up some of the details, but we know this battle actually happened. How? By discovering fossils. These two were actually fossilised in the very act of fighting! Roughly 70 million years later, in 1971, Polish palaeontologists were hunting for dinosaur fossils in the Gobi desert of Mongolia. They were amazed (gobsmacked, even) to find the skeleton of a *Velociraptor*, with its claws wrapped around the skull of a *Protoceratops*. It looks as though the two were fighting when a huge sandstorm came out of nowhere and rapidly buried them.

The struggle between the wily little hunter *Velociraptor* and the parrot-faced vegetarian *Protoceratops* is now the most famous of all dinosaur battles. It's the only example we know of a dinosaur battle frozen in time.

Other fights are harder to imagine, because we don't have all the evidence, but there are plenty of clues. Fossil experts have found bones with deep teeth marks or gouges, showing that some major wounds were inflicted. They've even found teeth broken off in the bones of victims, like the *Velociraptor* tooth described above. No pulling punches here. This was the daily life-and-death struggle for survival.

2

HOW DO WE KNOW ABOUT DINOSAURS?

We can see dinosaurs in movies or read about them in books. We can find images and information on dinosaurs on the Net. But where does all this information come from in the first place?

All the information we have comes from the study of fossils and rocks. Most of the world's dinosaur fossils are kept in museums, or sometimes in universities. Scientists go there to check facts about dinosaurs, or study them to find out new information.

WHAT ARE FOSSILS?

Fossils (from the Latin word meaning 'something that was dug up') are the remains of prehistoric creatures. They can be bones or teeth, eggs and nests, footprints or trail markings. But how are they preserved in the first place? Why don't they just rot away?

When an animal with a skeleton dies, birds or rats will usually chew at the bones. Then flies, worms, beetles and fungi will clean up what's left of the soft tissues – the meat and blood – covering the bones. Bacteria eat everything that's left, and this often starts the bone crumbling. If the bones are left outside in the weather, the hard part of the bone will eventually break up. Finally, nothing is left.

So how are fossil bones preserved? There are many ways, but here is a simple example.

First, the dinosaur must be buried by sand or mud, and fairly quickly, so that the bones aren't damaged or eaten. This can happen when an animal dies near a river, lake or sea, and its body is washed into the water by heavy rains. The body sinks to the bottom and is buried under dirt that washes into the river or lake. Then minerals in the mud or sand seep into the tiny holes in the bones and harden them.

Second, the layers of sand or mud must harden over time into sedimentary rocks – sandstone or mudstone.

A few fossil bones are almost perfectly preserved, without much change. More often, they look black and shiny, because they've been hardened by minerals. There are some in which the bone has been entirely replaced by opal! Sometimes the bones have been flattened (squashed) between layers of rock.

To find a *complete* dinosaur skeleton, we would need to find an ancient river or lake bed where the animal was buried whole. A flash flood can sweep up animals and drown them, and then the bones may stay together.

More often the animal falls into a river and the bones are washed downstream, so they become separated. The fossil remains will then be all jumbled up. This is the most common way that dinosaur bones are discovered. Palaeontologists (people who are experts on fossils) have to piece the bones back together, bit by bit, taking care to match them up with others from the same animal or species.

DINOSAUR EGGS

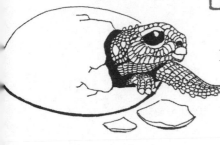

Fossilised dinosaur eggs and nests have been found in many parts of the world – China, India, Argentina and North America. The first dinosaur egg was found in southern France in 1869. The first complete dinosaur nest was found in Mongolia in the 1920s by famous American palaeontologist Roy Chapman Andrews.

We have eggs from almost all of the main types of dinosaurs that once lived on Earth.

Dinosaur eggs sometimes have the baby's bones inside them, so we can tell what kind of dinosaurs laid the eggs. We can also tell how some dinosaur parents looked after their babies (see pages 64–6).

DINOSAUR FOOTPRINTS

Dinosaur footprints are found throughout the world in special types of rock. Here's how it happens.

If a dinosaur walks along a river bank made of sand with a good amount of clay mixed in, it will leave deep, clear trackways.

Then the sun
bakes them hard.
The footprints are then gently
buried by blown sands, again and
again. Through time the footprint
layers harden and became rock
deep within the Earth. Much later,
through movements of the Earth's
crust, the layers of rock containing
the footprints are pushed back to the
surface. Erosion weathers away the
rock to expose the dinosaur tracks.
Trackways tell you all sorts
of things about dinosaurs that
bones cannot. The distance between
footprints can show how fast an animal is walking
or running. Here's a simple experiment to show you
what I mean.

SPEEDY OR SLOW?
THE FOOTPRINTS TELL

Next time you are down at the beach, walk along slowly in firm, damp sand to leave a clean set of footprints. Then go back and jog along beside them. Finally, sprint as fast as you can to leave a third trackway. Now look at how far apart each footprint is. Not only do your footprints get further apart as you run faster, but your prints get shallower. Only the front part of your foot touches the ground when you are running at full speed.

Scientists can estimate the speed of a running dinosaur from its fossilised trackways. First they work out the size of the animal from its footprints. The ratios of footprint size to foot size to total animal size are always the same for animals of a certain shape, including dinosaurs.
Next the scientists calculate whether it was walking, jogging or running at full speed.

The stresses on the ankle joints and leg bones of the dinosaur are greater as it gets bigger, so the really huge dinosaurs probably couldn't run fast. Still, a *Tyrannosaurus rex* could probably run at 17–25 kilometres an hour.

The fastest of all the dinosaurs were the ostrich mimics, the ornithomimosaurs. (Think of the *Gallimimus* herd in the movie *Jurassic Park*.) Dinosaur trackways tell us that the ornithomimosaurs could have run at speeds of between 60 and 110 kilometres an hour.

DINOSAUR SKIN

How about dinosaur skin? Is that ever preserved? Yes, in very rare cases the hard, baked skin of mummified dinosaurs can leave behind an impression in the mud or sands straight after the animal is buried. It works the same way as the footprints.

Some dinosaur-skin remains show small bony plates set into the skin. Other fossils, from a famous site in Liaoning, China, show clearly the imprints of short, hair-like feathers.

DINOSAUR POO

Poo (dung or 'faeces' as the scientists politely call it) can also be preserved as a fossil if it is hardened first by heat from the sun, and then is either buried by wind-blown sand or dust or falls into chemical-rich waters.

In some animals the chemicals already in their poo actually help to preserve it. A big plant-eating dinosaur, like a *Brachiosaurus*, would have had poo full of plant fibres. Such hard fibres help to preserve the poo, if it gets rapidly buried.

Fossilised dinosaur poo has a proper name – a coprolite (meaning 'poo stone'). *Tyrannosaurus* coprolites found in North America are full of tiny shards of bone. So we know that these big meat-eaters really did crunch up the bones of their prey.

FOSSILISED DINOSAUR ORGANS

Only a few years ago a most remarkable discovery
was made in North America. A dinosaur was found
with what seemed to be a fossilised heart preserved
inside its chest! The dinosaur, nicknamed 'Willy' by its
finders, was a *Thescelosaurus*, a plant-eater which grew
to about 4 metres long.

In another small dinosaur, *Scipionyx* from Italy,
the intestines and soft organs were preserved, squashed
flat between layers of very fine limestone. Minerals
must have rapidly formed around the decaying soft
tissues, replacing them with harder outlines of what
the soft organs once looked like.

So that's where our many pieces of evidence come
from. Palaeontologists not only dig up bones, they also
study footprints, eggs, nests, coprolites and rare soft
tissues. They are trained to use modern technology,
such as super-microscopes (electron microscopes),
and X-ray scanners (CT or CAT scanners) that build up
3D images of the insides of dinosaur skulls.

3

MEET THE
MEAT-EATERS

In 1902 a famous American palaeontologist named
Barnum Brown was busy searching the dry creek
beds of northern Montana, when he stumbled on
a real monster. Huge, saw-edged, dagger-like teeth
18 centimetres long stuck out of a jawbone nearly
a metre in length. After excavating the remains
of this part-skeleton, he was able to reconstruct
the largest and most terrifying meat-eater the
world had ever seen – *Tyrannosaurus rex*.

The meat-eating dinosaurs belong
to a group we've called theropods.

T-REX TOOTH ACTUAL SI

'Theropod' means 'beast-footed' because their feet looked like those of mammals to Professor Charles Marsh, who studied them.

The teeth of the meat-eating theropods are like steak knives, perfectly designed for cutting and tearing flesh. No other dinosaur family has teeth like them. Not all theropods ate meat, though. Some ate eggs, insects and other foods. These ones had small teeth or no teeth at all.

There were many different families of theropod dinosaur, and they ranged in size from a fully grown *Microraptor* only half a metre long to the giants like *Tyrannosaurus* and *Giganotosaurus*.

Coelurosaurs were smallish (for dinosaurs) and had long necks, five-fingered hands, and long snouts with many sharp teeth. Example: *Coelophysis* lived in North America 210 Mya (Triassic Period).

It was about the size of a tiger, at 1–3 metres, but probably ate lizards and insects. The coelurosaurs became extinct in the Cretaceous Period.

Allosaurids were medium-to-large (5–12 metres) predators with three-fingered hands and strong heads with bony knobs over their eyes. Examples are *Allosaurus* (North America, in the Jurassic period, about 150 Mya), and a close relative of *Allosaurus* (Australia, about 100 Mya), and *Sinraptor* (China).

Carcharodontosaurids were monstrous cousins of the allosaurids with serrated teeth like a Great White Shark. They included killers like *Carcharodontosaurus* in Africa, with a skull 1.9 metres long (it was even larger than *T. rex*), and *Giganotosaurus* (South America, up to 14 metres long , possibly weighing 8 tonnes). Both lived in the Cretaceous Period.

Giganotosaurus was probably the largest of all meat-eating dinosaurs – but of course the plant-eaters were many times bigger again, maybe *ten times* as heavy, as we'll see in the next chapter.

Tyrannosaurids include everyone's favourite dinosaur, the tyrant king *Tyrannosaurus rex*. *Siamotyrannus* (Thailand) and *Eotyrannus* (Isle of Wight, England) were both 7–8 metres long, and lived in the early Cretaceous Period (100 Mya). Most of the tyrannosaurs lived in Asia and North America during the late Cretaceous Period, 65–70 Mya. They were bigger than their forebears. *Tyrannosaurus* and its close cousins *Tarbosaurus* and *Ghengiskhan* were 12–14 metres long.

Tyrannosaurs had small arms with two tiny fingers. More importantly, they had forward-facing eyes, giving them keen eyesight – a big bonus for a hunter.

Spinosaurids had strange fins on their backs, and long, toothy snouts, rather like a crocodile. They loved to go fishing. Some examples are *Spinosaurus*, up to 15 metres long, and *Suchomimus*, 12 metres (both from northern Africa), and *Baryonyx* (England).

Baryonyx was the first fish-eating theropod to be described. It had huge curved claws on its hands, and a hooked snout which would have been handy for catching fish.

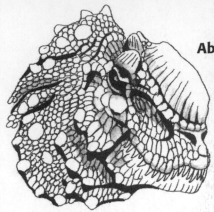

Abelisaurids were a really odd-looking group of medium-sized theropods, horned killers that lived mostly in the Southern Hemisphere. They were 5–7 metres long and had very small arms, three-fingered hands, and bony horns or domes on the head. Examples are *Carnotaurus* (Argentina), *Majungatholus* (Madagascar), and *Indosuchus* (India).

It's quite likely this group invaded Australia, but we haven't yet identified any of their bones in Australian fossil sites.

SPRINTERS

Ornithomimosaurs were the sprinters of the theropod world. They looked a lot like modern ostriches and had a long stiff tail to balance them when running. The earliest ones had teeth

(*Pelicanimimus* from Spain). Others just had a horny beak-like mouth (e.g. *Garudimimus*).

The oldest known fossil from this family comes from Australia. These are the thigh bones of a *Timimus* found in western Victoria.

Oviraptorids were wrongly labelled as 'egg robbers' (which is the meaning of *Oviraptor*) because of a spectacular discovery in Mongolia in the 1920s. Palaeontologists found the bones of an *Oviraptor* near a nest of dinosaur eggs, and thought this meant that it was stealing the eggs. New discoveries have shown that the eggs actually belonged to *Oviraptor*, so the animal was in fact sitting on its own nest.[1]

Oviraptorids probably ate insects and small animals. They may sometimes have eaten eggs of other animals. One oviraptor from China, *Incisivosaurus*, had a few flat buck teeth and probably ate plants. It may have lived like a rabbit in the dinosaur world.

---

[1] The word 'raptor' describes birds of prey, hawks and eagles, but in recent years it has been used to describe any of the small theropod dinosaurs with sickle claws.

Dromaeosaurids were theropods that are often called 'raptors' after *Velociraptor*. They had long arms and especially long fingers, retractable sickle claws on the feet, and razor-sharp hand claws.

Dromaeosaurids ranged in size from less than a metre (*Microraptor* from China) to 8 metres (giants like *Megaraptor* from South America).

The earliest member of this family could be *Ozraptor* in Western Australia (Middle Jurassic period, 175 Mya). By the early Cretaceous Period (120 Mya), several kinds had evolved. *Deinonychus* from Montana (North America) is a well-known one about 2 metres long. A group of *Deinonychus* skeletons was found buried with the remains of a big plant-eater, *Tenontosaurus*, which led scientists to suggest that they hunted in packs. That's probably the secret of their success.

Velociraptor lived in Mongolia and North America about 70 million years ago. You've already read about the one that died locked in battle with a *Protoceratops* (see pages 10–11).

Perhaps the weirdest-looking critter of the dinosaur world was *Therizinosaurus* from Mongolia. It was about 8 metres long, with a long neck and very small head. It walked upright on short, squat legs and its giant hooked claws hung down almost to the ground. These guys probably sat back on their broad hips and pulled palm fronds down with their huge claws so they could chew them with their rows of peg teeth. Only a few other therizinosaurid skeletons have been found, so we don't know much about them.

That's a quick rundown on theropods. And then there are the rest: 'theropod food'. Some of these plant-eaters grew to enormous sizes. Why? We'll answer that in the next chapter.

Greatest Ever Dinosaur Battles #2

Giganotosaurus v Antarctosaurus

It is 90 million years ago, in the steamy jungles of Argentina. The *Antarctosaurus* herd is busy eating ferns – a 30-metre-long sauropod is nearly always eating. There are about fifteen members of this herd, with three juveniles. These young ones are 6–9 metres long and are kept in the centre of the herd for safety. Thick bony plates on the backs of the adults give protection against most attackers. But will they be enough against *Giganotosaurus*?

At 14 metres long, *Giganotosaurus* is about the same length as a *T. rex*, but much heavier. Like *T. rex*, it is a meat-eater, one of the few large enough to prey on huge titanosaurids like *Antarctosaurus*.

The steamy jungle is warming up. Insects buzz around the trees, and some of the world's first flowers grow in the ground, along with colourful masses of fungi and lichens. The herd is noisily at work. Occasionally one rears up on its hind legs to push over a huge pine tree, opening up a new feeding area. Perhaps the crashing of falling trees and their own stomping stops the *Antarctosaurus* herd from hearing the ground shake as the massive meat-eater lumbers up the trail towards them.

Minutes later the *Giganotosaurus* sees its chance. A young sauropod has wandered further into the jungle to find a fresh feeding ground and it is now out of sight of the herd. The monster suddenly lunges out and grabs the little sauropod's neck in its huge jaws. It drags its dead victim into the forest and starts to feed.

The largest of the *Antarctosaurus* herd, a bull male, hears the dying cry of the juvenile. He bellows out a warning to the rest of the herd, and they huddle closer together.

The *Giganotosaurus* continues feeding, until it hears the ground quaking. It turns, to see the huge *Antarctosaurus* rear up on its hind legs, swishing arm claws menacingly. Then, with unexpected speed, it whips its body around and smacks the *Giganotosaurus* with its huge tail. The many rows of sharp bony spikes in the tail draw a line of blood across the predator's body. *Giganotosaurus* roars, as the *Antarctosaurus* lifts its head up high and turns its body around, making itself safe from any attack.

The bleeding *Giganotosaurus* rushes forward, trying to bite the hind leg of the sauropod. But the sauropod is unexpectedly fast. It knocks the giant predator to the ground, using its long powerful neck, and then delivers the final blow. Its unforgiving weight crushes *Giganotosaurus*'s 2-metre-long head like a ripe melon, killing it instantly.

The sauropod then turns and walks to where the dead youngster lies. It nuzzles the body of its young calf, the only young male in the herd. It pulls some branches down from the nearby trees with its teeth, and gently covers the body. Next year another breeding cycle will begin. Life will go on as usual. And, as usual, death will follow closely.

4

WORLD'S BIGGEST (AND DUMBEST?) VEGETARIANS

The sauropods (meaning 'lizard-footed') were the largest animals ever to walk the face of the Earth. *Apatosaurus*, which used to be called *Brontosaurus*, is a well-known example.[2] This animal lived in North America about 150 million years ago, was up to

---

[2] *Brontosaurus* means 'thunder lizard' – because of its gigantic farts? It did eat a lot of plant material, after all. Because of a bone mix-up, the name was changed to *Apatosaurus* ('deceptive reptile').

21 metres long and weighed around 25 tonnes. It had a small head, long neck and tail, and very large body. Sauropods all have this same kind of body plan, but some differ in the shape of their teeth or claws. Some had armoured plates set in their skin, or sharp spines down their backs.

Careful study of sauropod skeletons revealed that they were land animals that fed mostly on ferns. Most would have walked with their necks stretched forward, balancing the long tail. Perhaps they knocked down trees using their huge bulk to get to fresh fern glades and eat the tender shoots on top of the trees, as African elephants do today.

Why did they get so big? Partly because there was lots of food, and partly because the big ones were better able to protect themselves from the meat-eaters, and so they survived and had children.

BIGGEST OF THE BIG

The **heaviest** of all the sauropods was probably *Argentinosaurus* (South America, about 90 Mya).

Its thighbone measures 2.5 metres. By comparing such bones with other complete sauropod skeletons, we can guess that it was 35–40 metres long and weighed as much as 70 or 80 tonnes. *Antarctosaurus* weighed about the same.

The **longest**, but not the heaviest, of all sauropods was *Seismosaurus* from New Mexico in North America. The name means 'ground-shaking lizard', and we think *Seismosaurus* was at least 39 and maybe as much as 52 metres long. (We're not sure if the one well-preserved skeleton that we have belonged to a young *Seismosaurus* or a fully grown one.)

DUMBEST OF THE DUMB?

The one drawback sauropods had is that in growing so large they seem to have left their brains behind! Sauropod brains were really small, the smallest of any dinosaur family. This doesn't mean that they were really stupid, though. Think about these facts:

➤ Whales have brains far larger than humans, but we are far more intelligent.

➤ In animals that don't run fast, parts of the brain are smaller, as the sense of balance doesn't have to be so well developed.

➤ A smaller brain uses up a lot less energy.[3]

We believe now that sauropods functioned effectively with a small brain, as most of the animal was sheer bulk.

[3] Did you know that koalas have very small brains? – just as well, because gumleaves don't provide much energy!

HIP DINO

Scientists once believed that some sauropods had
a second brain in their hips, but we now know that
this is not true. They did have an enlarged area inside
the hip bone, but it's more likely this contained a gland
to regulate hormones, as in some modern birds.

KEEP OFF, OR ELSE!

Sauropods might look as though they had no real
defence against predators, but they had several ways
of protecting themselves from attack.

Most of them had well-developed hand or foot
claws and could slash viciously at any attackers.

They all had long, heavy tails which could deal
a powerful blow to any foe. Some had a hard, bony club
on the end of the tail.

They could occasionally rear up on their hind limbs and crash down on top of attacking theropods, crushing them under their huge weight.

Some sauropods had sharp rows of spikes along their backs (e.g. *Diplodocus*, *Amargasaurus*) or armoured plates of bone set in the skin (e.g. *Saltasaurus*).

Sauropod trackways show that their usual defence against hungry predators was to herd together, with the biggest animals on the outside of the group, the youngest and weakest in the centre.

WHALE LIZARDS AND WHIP-LIKE TAILS

The earlier sauropods lived in the Jurassic Period.

Cetiosaurids, not surprisingly, included *Cetiosaurus* (meaning 'whale lizard') from England. One cetiosaur, *Shunosaurus* from China, had a bony club on the end of its tail so it could whack its attackers for six!

Brachiosaurids are among the heaviest sauropods we've found so far. *Brachiosaurus* was about 25 metres long and weighed up to 60 tonnes. Its bones have been found in Africa, North America and possibly Australia.

Camarasaurids had a short, bulldog-type muzzle, and had slightly larger hind legs than front legs. *Camarasaurus* was one of the commonest dinosaurs known from the Jurassic in North America. It grew to about 18 metres long.

Diplodocids had very long necks and whip-like tails. Some scientists believe that diplodocids could crack their long whip-like tails to create loud sound waves to scare away attackers. *Diplodocus* and *Amargasaurus* also had rows of sharp spikes along their backs and big claws on their hands. *Diplodocus* lived in North America and reached 27 metres long, but its cousin *Seismosaurus* was much larger, perhaps 52 metres.

Mamenchisaurus is the largest dinosaur from China so far known, at 25 metres long.

ARMOURED GOLIATHS

Other kinds of sauropods appeared in the Cretaceous Period.

Titanosaurids were the last sauropods to survive in most of the southern continents.

They include the heaviest dinosaurs of all, such as *Argentinosaurus* and *Antarctosaurus* (perhaps 35 metres long and 80 tonnes). Armoured *Saltasaurus* was another titanosaurid.

5

WEAPONS OF DESTRUCTION OR DEFENCE: HORNS AND ARMOUR

The long-necked sauropods may have used their massive size to protect themselves, but many other plant-eating dinosaurs had their own ways of fending off attackers. In fact, it was very difficult for any attacker to even get close to them. In this chapter we meet two such groups of dinosaurs:

The **thyreophorans** (meaning 'shield-bearers') include the armour-plated ankylosaurs and the back-plated, tail-horned stegosaurs.

The **marginocephalians** include the well-known ceratopsians, and the dome-headed pachycephalosaurs.

Both are bird-hipped dinosaurs (see page 9).

They may have big names, but they are easy to recognise once you see what they look like!

ARMOURED PLANT- EATERS

Ankylosaurids were the 'tanks' of the dinosaur world. They were heavily armoured, with thick bony plates in their skin, scutes (small bony plates set in the skin, like the scales on a crocodile) and sharp spines sticking out along the sides of their bodies, and sometimes with a solid bony club on the end of the tail.

The ankylosaurids had a very good sense of smell, as shown by well-developed tubes inside the snout part of their skulls. The ankylosaurids had triangular heads, usually adorned with large spines. The largest ones lived in North America, during the late Cretaceous Period: *Ankylosaurus* (10 metres long) and *Euoplocephalus* (7 metres).

Stegosaurids were four-legged plant-eaters, with small front arms and large hind legs. They usually had rows of armoured plates or spikes on the back and tail for defence. The heads were small and they had many small teeth. Like the sauropods, stegosaurids were once thought to have a second brain in their hips, but scientists have now decided it was just a gland. *Stegosaurus* (North America, late Jurassic), is the best-known member of this group. Others include *Tuojiangosaurus* (China, Jurassic Period) and *Dravidosaurus* (India, late Cretaceous Period).

We know that stegosaurids lived in Australia too, because there are fossilised hand- and footprints preserved at Broome, Western Australia.

HORNED AND DOMED PLANT- EATERS

The marginocephalians include some of the best-known of all dinosaurs, like *Triceratops*. These horned dinosaurs, called ceratopsians, were really the rhinos of the dinosaur world. They had many hundreds of small teeth growing out of each jaw for chewing hard plant fibres. Many of them had elaborate frills around the skull to protect their necks from predators' attacks.

Protoceratops, living in the late Cretaceous Period, is a good example of an early ceratopsian. It was about 2 metres long.

So many *Protoceratops* bones have been found in Mongolia that some scientists have called them the 'sheep of the dinosaur world'.

The larger ceratopsians dominated North America and Asia in late Cretaceous times. These include large animals growing to 7 metres long like *Triceratops*, with three large horns, *Styracosaurus*, which had a frill armed with horns, and *Centrosaurus* with a single long nose-horn. *Torosaurus* is also a famous ceratopsian, as it had the largest skull of any land animal (2.5 metres long).

Some ceratopsians lived in huge herds. Large numbers of *Centrosaurus* skeletons have been found in Canada at many sites, indicating that a giant herd of some 10 000 dinosaurs may have roamed the plains there 70 million years ago. A flash flood probably drowned them all.

Pachycephalosaurids were upright, walking, dome-headed plant-eaters. They had very strong necks and backbones – perhaps they used their solid bony heads for ramming each other during mating battles. *Pachycephalosaurus* grew to 8 metres long and had a thick skull with a plate of bone nearly 20 centimetres thick. This would have deflected shock waves away from the rest of its skeleton whenever it rammed an opponent. *Stygimoloch* was smaller, about 6 metres long, with large spikes jutting out around the rim of its head. It too had a very thick, domed skull. Both lived in North America in late Cretaceous times, about 70 million years ago.

6

A BUNCH OF WEIRD WEED-MUNCHERS

Some types of dinosaurs had no form of obvious defence against predators. Fabrosaurids and heterodontosaurids were small (1–2 metres), agile dinosaurs that lived mostly in the late Triassic and could run on their hind legs or graze on all fours. Later on, in Cretaceous times, came the duck-billed hadrosaurs, the thumb-spiked iguanodonts and the little hypsilophodontids and dryosaurids. None of them had horns on their head or sharp spikes on their backs. Perhaps they relied on the herd approach to safety, just like zebras and antelopes today.

(This would also help to explain the large number of their bones found at some fossil sites in Canada and North America.) When stalked by a big meat-eating dinosaur, like a *T. rex*, they would scatter and run away, knowing that only one of them would be taken by the hunter.

Nearly all of these dinosaurs had the same body type: large hind legs, smaller front arms, and a narrow head with many small teeth good for chewing on woody food.

RUN LIKE A DEER

Hypsilophodontids were the deer or gazelles of the dinosaur world. They were swift and lightly built and smallish (most were 1–2 metres in length, except for *Tenontosaurus*, which was 7 metres). We used to think that *Hypsilophodon*, which lived on the Isle of Wight during the Early Cretaceous, was a tree-climbing dinosaur. More recent studies of its skeleton show that it was a fast runner and lived in forest. One Australian hypsilophodontid, *Leaellynasaura*, had very large eyes

and was probably well adapted to living in a cold polar forest with three months of the year in darkness.

THUMB-KNIVES AND THEIR KIN

The iguanodonts (meaning 'iguana-tooth') are so called because of early studies that compared their teeth with those of the living iguana lizards. *Iguanodon*, the best-known member of the group, lived in Europe

and North America during the early
Cretaceous period. Up to 10 metres long,
it had a sharp thumb-spike on each hand
which could be jabbed into the throat of any
attacker. Although *Iguanodon* and its relatives could
walk comfortably on their large hind legs, they could
also rest (and maybe run) on all fours. Their hands had
large flat fingers that could act like hooves and dig into
the ground. *Ouranosaurus* was a spectacular-looking
iguanodont with a sail-like fin on its back. It may have
used this to take in heat from the sun to warm its
body on cold days. It lived in northern Africa in a
climate that was dry and warm, but probably had very
cold nights.

Muttaburrasaurus from Australia was once labelled
an iguanodont and *Muttaburrasaurus* skeletons were
often reassembled with a thumb-spike on each hand.

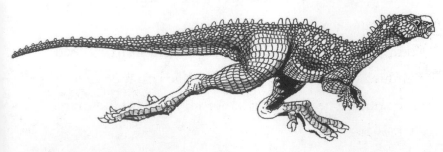

New studies have shown that there was never any evidence for the thumb-spike and that because it had a weird bump on its snout, and its teeth were unlike those of *Iguanodon*, it wasn't actually related to this family. *Muttaburrasaurus* grew to 10 metres long and probably used its snout bump to inflate skin around the nose, bellowing out warnings to the rest of its herd when danger was near.

DAFFY DUCKBILLS

The hadrosaurids or duckbills were a group of large, upright, plant-eating dinosaurs in the late Cretaceous Period. They had many thousands (yes, thousands) of small teeth which grew continuously from the jaws. Clearly these teeth were a special adaptation useful for chewing on tough plants. Some of the duckbills had strange bony structures on top of their heads, like helmets, crests or spikes. Such structures are connected to the nasal tubes inside the animal's head and must have helped them to make trumpeting noises for communicating with other members of the herd.

Examples are *Corythosaurus*, *Parasaurolophus* and the Chinese hadrosaurid, *Tsintaosaurus*.

The hadrosaurids are known from some of the most spectacular fossils ever found – mummified dinosaurs, discovered in southern Canada. These fossils show the complete skeleton in the death position, with marks of the skin still stuck to rocks around the dinosaur's body. They had a fine leathery skin, lacking any hard bony plates.

Greatest Ever Dinosaur Battles #3

Tyrannosaurus v Triceratops

We have travelled to the plains of North America, 66 million years ago.

In the distance, high up on a ledge, is 14-metre *Tyrannosaurus rex*, the largest meat-eating dinosaur in the whole continent. Down in the valley a large herd of *Triceratops* is grazing. In these numbers they have little to fear. Any stalking predator would surely be sniffed

out by one of them. Like rhinoceroses, *Triceratops* have two main defences: their horns, and their keen sense of smell.

The *T. rex* is cunning. He moves downwind of the herd, behind some trees, so that none of them can see or smell him. He lowers his huge body to ground level and creeps forward on his haunches, his belly rubbing the ground. The top of his head is well hidden by the 2-metre-high scrub. He is now only metres way from a lone *Triceratops*, chewing its cud.

A sudden change of wind direction blows the scent of the huge predator towards the unwary *Triceratops*. Immediately it stops chewing and trumpets a warning to the rest of the herd. Too late. With a mighty rush, the 6-tonne carnivore launches itself on the *Triceratops*, sinking deadly 15-centimetre teeth into its back. Red blood gushes from the wound. The *Triceratops* manages to roll around underneath and thrust its three large horns into the attacker's side. The *T. rex* screeches in pain, but the wound is not deadly. It rips open *Triceratops'* stomach. As steaming innards pile out, the *T. rex* begins to feed. Blood smears all over its teeth and face.

Suddenly, there is a deafening roar. The giant predator jerks its head around in time to see the *Triceratops* herd charging straight at it. The angry mob stampedes across *T. rex*, crushing it to death.

In late Cretaceous times, there was no such thing as an easy meal!

7

DINOSAUR RUSTLERS AND SMUGGLERS

You've heard of cattle rustling – in Australia it's sometimes called cattle duffing. Some cowboy steals your cattle and covers up the brand. Well, dinosaur rustling has been going on since the days of the wild, wild west in the USA. Of course I don't mean rustling live dinosaurs – I'm talking about the theft of dinosaur skeletons. It began with the 'bones wars' . . .

In the 1880s, teams of fossil-hunters went out to search for dinosaur bones in Wyoming and Utah, armed with guns to ward off attacking Indians. When a new dinosaur site was discovered, it was jealously guarded. Sometimes a group would raid another group's site, where bones were marked out ready to be dug up, and steal the bones in the night. At times they even blew up the opposition's dig site with dynamite to destroy the competition!

Dinosaur fossils of any kind are worth a lot of money. The *Tyrannosaurus rex* skeleton known as 'Sue' was dug up in South Dakota in 1990 and sold at a public auction in 1997 for US$8 million (around $14 million Australian).[4] The people who dug it up claimed they owned it. So did the rancher whose land it was on, and the Indians who had part claim on the area, and the US Goverment! The bones were seized in a raid by the FBI, and there was a court case to decide who should keep the skeleton. The judge finally decided that the rancher had the best claim, and the rancher then put Sue up for sale at an auction.

[4] Sue was bought by a museum in Chicago, using money given by McDonald's and Disney.

Dinosaur smuggling is a world-wide problem, and it's growing. In China, all dinosaur fossils (including fossilised eggs) are protected. It's illegal to export them to other countries or sell them on open markets. But many are dug out when authorities are not watching, and secretly taken out of the country. They then appear for sale at international fossil shows in America or Europe and are sold to buyers who don't know they've been smuggled. In the US, too, poachers sometimes come in and dig up dinosaur fossils to sell. If they are caught, they can be heavily fined or jailed.

FOSSIL HOTSPOTS

Liaoning, northern China

This is the most exciting dinosaur site on the planet for small dinosaurs and birds. Wonderful fossils (including feathers and soft tissue) from early Cretaceous times (130 Mya) are preserved in an ancient lake bed. Teams of scientists are busy working this site.

Argentina, South America

Neuquen Province has some of the most spectacular large dinosaur fossils yet known from the Cretaceous period. Among them are the fearsome *Giganotosaurus*, a carnivore that was heavier than *T. rex* (read all about it in Greatest Ever Dinosaur Battles #2!) and the horned predator *Carnotaurus*.

South Dakota, USA

This is where the full *T. rex* skeleton, nicknamed 'Sue', was found in 1992. Recently, collectors Fred and Candy Nuss found a new kind of giant oviraptorosaur and it's up for sale, for US $1 million.

Dinosaur Cove, Australia

Dinosaur Cove in western Victoria has yielded more dinosaur bones than any other site in Australia. Amazingly, these dinosaurs lived in a cold polar environment within the Antarctic Circle, about 100 million years ago.

It's hard to prevent fossil crime. The sites are often quite remote, on government reserve lands or in national parks. In Australia we had a famous theft of rare dinosaur footprints from a beach near Broome, Western Australia, in 1996. The prints were the only ones known in Australia of stegosaurid dinosaurs. The theft was illegal because it was from a protected fossil site on Crown (government) land. It was also against Aboriginal law, as the local people had their own legends about the dinosaur footprints and it was a sacred site. I was part of a team that tried to track down the thief and return the fossil, but we never found out who the criminal was. (My book *The Dinosaur Dealers* tells the full story.)

Another dinosaur print stolen from Broome was recovered in 1999, and a man was arrested and jailed for the theft.

Fossil crime takes many forms. Dinosaur bones are not only poached and smuggled — some are copied. Illegal fake fossils are a huge industry because many buyers can't tell if they are getting a real fossil or a man-made one. Most of the best fossil fakes come from Morocco or China.

To test whether something is a real bone or a fake, you need to examine it close up under a hand lens, looking for bone structure. You should also try to cut a tiny bit with a blade to see if it's made of plastic or resin.

STOP PRESS Just as this book was going to press, the Australian Federal Police seized 20 tonnes of fossils illegally brought in from China to Western Australia. Most of the fossils came from the sites in Liaoning Province. There were 3500 fossils – dinosaur eggs, nests, skulls, fish, mammal skulls – dating back to 130 million years ago. They were valued at close to $4 million.

The penalty for anyone convicted of importing fossils from a country whose laws prohibit this is up to $100 000 *per item*, or five years in jail.

8

INSIDE DINOSAUR DAILY LIVES

What do we really know about the day-to-day lives of dinosaurs? Some neat new evidence has turned up in recent years, giving us some new insights into dinosaur behaviour.

RAISING THE CHILDREN

Egg Mountain in Montana, North America, is a world-famous dinosaur fossil site. American palaeontologist Jack Horner discovered a dinosaur nesting ground there with well-preserved nests and eggs. Some of the eggs contained the skeletons of baby dinosaurs, and near them were bones of newly hatched ones. Dr Horner discovered that the baby dinosaur leg bones had not fully hardened, so they would have had to rely on the parent to bring food to them in the nest for maybe 6–8 weeks. The dinosaur which made these nests was named *Maiasaura*, meaning 'good mother lizard'.

Fossil skeletons of the small theropod *Oviraptor* have been found in Mongolia actually sitting on top of their own nest, brooding the eggs. The mother dinosaurs were crouched over the circular nest, with arms outstretched to cover it. A sudden sandstorm must have rapidly buried them alive. Finds like this make the link between birds and dinosaurs even clearer.

DINOSAUR LOVE

Before laying eggs, dinosaurs had to find a mate. Studies of some dinosaur skulls, like those of pachycephalosaurs, strongly suggest that the males would have fought over the best females in the herd. Meat-eating theropods often had rough patches of bone above the eyes which may have been used for head-to-head pushing battles between the big males. The hadrosaurs' bony crests could have been displayed to attract females, especially if colourful webs of skin adorned them.

Dinosaurs mated in much the same way as modern birds or reptiles. The male inserted his penis (or penes – some reptiles and birds have two) inside the female, to shed sperm onto the eggs. The female then laid the fertilised eggs in a nest and waited for them to hatch. The fossil tail bones of one large sauropod shows that its tail could have moved sideways to a fair degree. If it was a female, then this would have enabled the male to get close enough to mate with it. Pressure on the backs of sauropod females must have been great during mating, as the gargantuan male would have to rest on the female's back to get close enough to mate.

SICK DAYS

Like all animals, us included, dinosaurs got sick from time to time. Some of their fossil bones show evidence of infection. One bone from a small hypsilophodontid dinosaur found in Victoria showed that the bone grew crooked after a deep wound was inflicted on the animal. Such cases indicate that the animal was badly injured after an attack, but it had enough time to rest and let its wounds heal without being attacked again.

Actually, dinosaur injuries are very rarely detected in their fossil bones. Parasites which sucked the blood of dinosaurs must have existed, as they do on all large animals today. Some ankylosaur bony plates that were set into the skin show circular depressions which some scientists think were caused by burrowing parasites, because they are identical to wounds found in living turtles with shell parasites.

Other fossils that indicate dinosaurs sometimes got sick include cases of arthritis in the ankle bones of the huge plant-eater *Iguanodon* found in Belgium. Arthritis is a painful disease caused by abnormal bone growth.

T. REX OR T. REGINA?

How do we know which dinosaurs were male or female? When we study the skeletons of modern reptiles like crocodiles, we discover that females lack

certain bones in
the tail area.
This made
room for
the large
oviduct organ,
in which the
eggs were laid.
In the same
way, the long

pubis bone is curved in females to allow room for the
eggs. (It's straight in male crocodiles.) The same is
true of *Tyrannosaurus rex* skeletons. Interestingly, the
female *Tyrannosaurus* was slightly bigger and more
robust than the male. This is often the case where
females must defend the nest and ward off any danger,
including threats from the male of their own species.

Male and female differences have also been
suggested for some of the crested duck-billed
dinosaurs. The males apparently had larger and
showier crests on top of their heads than the females,
although we need more examples to show if this is true.

9

DINOSAURS TAKE TO THE AIR

In the late 1860s, a fossilised bird from the late
Jurassic Period was discovered
in Germany. Although it still
had a reptile-like tail and body,
the feathers coming out of its
arms clearly identified it
as a bird. It was named
Archaeopteryx (meaning
'ancient wing') and for the last
130 years has been widely used as a
good example of a primitive bird.

However, in the last 10 years we have seen a number of exciting new discoveries come out of the early Cretaceous sites in Liaoning, China. These sites contain the world's best-preserved dinosaurs – some with feathers clearly visible on their bodies and limbs.

DINOSAURS OF A FEATHER

The first discovery of a feathered dinosaur from China was announced in 1996. This was *Sinosauropteryx*, a small coelurosaur about a metre long. Its head and body was covered with fine, unbranched feathers,

proving once and for all that feathers were not unique to birds. Since then a number of other dinosaurs from China, including early dromaeosaurids, therizinosaurids and oviraptorosaurs, have been found with feathers on them.

PREPARING FOR TAKE- OFF

Some of these early feathered dinosaurs from China show the first steps required for a dinosaur to evolve into a true bird.

Caudipteryx, for example, has long feathers on the arms which are branched, forming small wings on its forearms. The wings were way too small to be used for flying, so *Caudipteryx* must have been halfway between a small running dinosaur and a bird. It probably used its mini wings for trapping flying insects.

Microraptor, a small feathered dromaeosaurid, has been nicknamed the 'four-winged dinosaur' because it has long feathers on its arms as well as wing-like feathers on its legs. It was probably able to glide from tree to tree.

These dinosaurs probably lived in trees, where they could hunt insects and lizards that were out of reach for other hunters. Feathers not only provided insulation and warmth, but enabled them to glide.

The ones that had longer 'fingers' and wider wings would have been better at gliding, and more likely to survive and reproduce.

Gradually the species developed bigger and better wings, along with stronger breast muscles to flap the wings, and a higher heartbeat to sustain the energy needed for flight.

One large theropod from South America called *Unenlargia* had developed a special kind of wrist that must have helped it grab its prey in a certain way. This modified wrist was the forerunner to being able to fold the wing back.

DINOBIRDS RULE!

Some of the earliest true birds are known from early Cretaceous fossils found at the Chinese sites in Liaoning. Some had lost the teeth and developed typical bird-like beaks. Others had developed a very strong chest bone (sternum) with a keel for breast muscle attachment. The loss of the long bones of the tail lightened the skeleton, and the hip bone became specially modified in order to brace the sudden shock of landing when the bird stopped flying. Some, like *Confuciusornis*, even show different feather patterns in males and females. We think that the birds with very long tufted tail feathers are the males, as modern male birds are generally showier than females (e.g. peacocks).

Once birds had hit on their winning formula for flight, nothing could stop them. They began to spread out across the globe, and had soon evolved into many new species. By the end of the Cretaceous Period, as the land dinosaurs were about to become extinct, there were about 100 species of true birds.

These birds are all around us today, the only living survivors of the dinosaur family. So it's true – the dinosaurs never died!

10

DOWNFALL OF THE DINOSAURS

So why did most of the dinosaurs die out? It's a
question we may never really know the answer to,
as evidence is scarce. Here are some of the
most likely explanations.

THEORY 1 : HIT BY A METEORITE

Some scientists believe that a massive meteorite
smashed into the Earth just south of Mexico, 65 million
years ago, when most dinosaurs became extinct.
Just imagine a rock 10 kilometres wide smashing into

the planet at a speed of about 11 kilometres per second. Masses of ash and dust would have spewed high into the upper atmosphere, probably blocking the sun's rays for several months. This would stop plants from growing and cause havoc for plant-eating animals of all kinds, and then for meat-eaters that relied on eating the plant-eaters.

We are fairly sure that a meteorite did crash into the Earth at this time, but the theory still doesn't explain why dinosaurs became extinct while several other groups of animals and plants managed to survive. Frogs, lizards, turtles, crocodiles, birds and mammals survived the devastating impact at the end of the Cretaceous, yet all land-dwelling dinosaurs and flying pterosaurs died. Perhaps they were simply too reliant on particular foods, and unable to find other food sources when the weather changed.

THEORY 2: CLIMATE CHANGE

Earth became colder at the end of the Cretaceous Period and plant growth became less reliable. This was bad news for the animals that fed on the plants. Sea levels also rose towards the end of the Cretaceous, flooding the low-lying coastal plains which were usually lush jungles full of plants. Flowering plants appeared for the first time, gradually replacing the forests of pines and other conifers by the end of the Cretaceous Period. Some of these new plants produced poisons that stopped animals eating them. Perhaps the plant-eating dinosaurs couldn't deal with these new-fangled plants.

The problem with this theory is that it describes quite gradual change. It doesn't really explain why dinosaurs should die out suddenly, rather than fade off in a series of gradual extinctions.

THEORY 3: VOLCANIC DESTRUCTION

Another theory is that at the end of the Cretaceous Period there was a huge amount of volcanic activity. Large volcanic eruptions fling ash high into the atmosphere, blocking the sun and disrupting the growth of plants. Lava flows could have wiped out dinosaur nesting grounds and destroyed forests.

We know there were volcanic eruptions at the right time in some places, like India. But for this idea to be accepted, we would need to have much more evidence of widespread volcanic activity at the same time all around the world.

The truth is that we don't really know what killed the dinosaurs. Perhaps it was a combination of all three things, climate change, volcanic explosions and finally a meteorite or asteroid crashing into the Earth – maybe the final straw that broke the sauropod's back!

HOW TO FIND YOUR OWN FOSSILS

FINDING DINOSAUR FOSSILS ISN'T EASY, BUT HERE ARE A FEW HANDY TIPS.

Find the right rocks Dinosaurs lived in the Mesozoic Era, so rocks 225 to 65 million years old are the ones to go for. We also know that most dinosaur fossils are found in sedimentary rocks deposited in ancient rivers or lakes.

Find a rock mapper You might be able to get hold of a map of your area showing rock types, but the map will only be helpful if you know someone who is trained to read a geological map correctly. Geologists can often be contacted through your local natural history museum, or through geology departments at most universities. Be sure to ask for a specialist in Mesozoic sedimentary rocks!

Get the OK from the landowner You need permission to look for fossils on their land.

Pack the correct tools You will need hammers and chisels, and possibly a pick for digging large holes, plus wrapping paper, plaster of paris and cloth to pack your finds.

Know what to look for Remember, fossilised bones often look nothing like modern bone. They can be black or brown in colour, and may have turned to stone, because of minerals seeping into them.

WHAT TO DO IF YOU FIND FOSSIL BONE

Take a small piece of the bone, wrap it up carefully and bring it in to your local museum. If you have found a real dinosaur bone, the museum palaeontologists will want to see the site and organise the excavation properly. They know how to dig it up without damaging any of the bones. Fossilised bones are often very brittle and easy to break.

CAN FOSSIL-HUNTING BE A JOB?

Jobs in palaeontology do not come up very often, and they are mostly in museums or universities. Micro-palaeontologists study micro-fossils and help mining companies searching for oil, gas or mineral deposits. Studying fossils also helps us to understand climate changes.

ANSWERS TO THE QUIZ ON PAGE 1

True

True (probably)

False, only distantly related

True

False, some dinosaurs survived – the birds;
the rest died out (maybe because of a meteorite)

False (only about half of the dinosaurs were
bigger than a cow)

False, some lived in very cold places

PRONUNCIATION GUIDE

Names that are very well known or easy to work out aren't listed here.

abelisaurids Ab-el-ee-saw-rids
ankylosaurids an-kill-o-
Antarctosaurus Ant-ark-to-
Archaeopteryx Ar-kee-op-ter-ix
Argentinosaurus Ar-jen-teen-o-
Baryonyx Barry-on-ix
Brachiosaurus brack-ee-o-
Carcharodontosaurus Car-car-o-dont-o-
Caudipteryx Caw-di-ter-ix (silent p)
Coelophysis See-lo-fy-sis
coelurosaurs See-lure-o-
Confuciusornis Con-few-shus-or-nis
Corythosaurus Cor-eeth-o-
Deinonychus Di-no-ny-kus
dromaeosaurids dro-may-o-
Euoplochephalus Ew-o-plo-keff-a-lus
Gallimimus Gall-ee-my-muss
Ghenghiskhan Gen-gis-kahn
Giganotosaurus Guy-ga-note-o-
hypsilophodontids hip-sill-off-o-don-tids
Iguanodon Ig-yu-ah-no-don
Indosuchus In-doe-sue-kus
Leaellynosaura Lee-ell-ee-na-
Maiasaura My-a-
Majungatholus Ma-jun-go-thol-us
Mamenchisaurus Ma-men-chee-

marginocephalians mar-jin-o-keff-alians
ornithomimosaurs aw-nith-o-my-mo-
Ouranosaurus Oo-ran-o-
oviraptorids ov-ee-rap-to-rids
pachycephalosaurids pack-ee-keff-al-o-
palaeontologists pal-lee-on-tol-o-jists
Parasaurolophus Para-saw-rol-o-fuss
Pelecanimimus Pel-ee-can-ee-my-muss
pterosaurs terr-o- (silent p)
saurischians saw-rish-ee-ans
Seismosaurus Size-mo-
Shunosaurus Shun-o-
Siamotyrannus Sy-am-o-tie-ran-us
Sinosauropteryx Sine-o-saw-rop-ter-ix
Sinraptor Sine-rap-tor
Spinosaurids Spy-no-
Stygimoloch Stij-ee-mo-lock
Styracosaurus Sty-rack-o-
Suchomimus Sue-ko-my-muss
thecodonts theek-o-donts
Therezinosaurus Ther-ree-zine-o-
Thescelosaurus Thess-ell-o-
thyreophorans thy-re-off-or-ans
Timimus Tim-my-muss
Tsintaosaurus Chin-tow-
Tuojiangosaurus Tor-jang-o-
Velociraptor vel-oss-ee-raptor

JOHN LONG began collecting fossils at the age of seven. He has collected fossils in Australia, Thailand, Vietnam and South Africa, and has been on two expeditions to Antarctica.

John says his home computer is covered in small plastic dinosaurs. 'When I get bored, the *T. rex* always starts attacking the hadrosaur! That's how I started writing about the greatest ever dinosaur battles.'

John's hobbies include writing, reading, drawing, motorcycles and martial arts. He works at the Western Australia Museum in Perth.

TRAVIS TISCHLER How could I not love dinosaurs, when I grew up in Texas? There are dino bones everywhere there, and I was fascinated by them. As a kid, I always loved drawing and making model dinosaurs. I still do! – but now the models are bigger and I get paid for making them.

THANKS

Many thanks to Travis Tischler for his drawings, and to Heather
Robinson for helping with the editing of this book. I give
thanks to the many colleagues in dinosaur research who have
given me help and information over the years, especially
Professor Pat Vickers-Rich and Dr Tom Rich, Dr Ralph Molnar
and Dr Tony Thulborn.

John Long

The publishers would like to thank the following for
photographs used in the text: Glenn Martin for those on pages
i, 60, 65, 71; Anon. for the one on page 42; Greg Wallace, WA
Museum, for the one on page 55; Steve Morton, Thomas Rich
and Patricia Vickers-Rich for the ones on pages 15 and 81;
the Queensland Museum for the one on page 79; and John
Long for those on pages vii, 8, 13, 20, 48, 61, 62, 69, 75, 82
(based on a model built by Travis Tischler in the WA Museum).

WHERE TO FIND OUT MORE

Not everything you read or find out about dinosaurs is true.

Books

Look for books that are up-to-date. It's best if they are dated 1995 or later. Your local museum bookshop is a good place to start. Check the author blurb to find out if the author really is an expert. Here are some suggestions:

David Norman and Angela Milner, *Eyewitness Guide to Dinosaurs*, Dorling Kindersley (first issued in 1989, updated several times – look for the most recent edition)

Barbara Taylor, *The Really Deadly and Dangerous Dinosaurs, and other monsters of the prehistoric world*, Dorling Kindersley, 1997

Paul Willis (consultant editor), *The Little Guides – Dinosaurs*, Fog

Museums

Almost all museums and some university geology departments in major cities will have fossils on display.

Most modern museums also have good websites with detailed information about their collections. Some have discovery centres or question-and-answer desks for dealing with your enquiries. They often have great bookshops.

Websites

Many websites that have information about dinosaurs are inaccurate and out of date. There are some very strange creationist sites that deliberately put out wrong information on dinosaurs, so be careful! (Ask your teacher what 'creationist' means.) The ones you can trust are sites put up by museums and universities that do research on dinosaurs and fossils, or sites that these institutions highly recommend.

- www.ucmp.berkeley.edu/diapsids/dinosaur.html
- www.geocities.com/stegob/dinoland.html
- www.dinosauricon.com/
- www.isgs.uiuc.edu/dinos/dinos_home.htm

For teachers

M.K. Brett-Surman (ed.), C. Brochu, J. Long, C. McHenry, J.D. Scanlon & P. Willis, *Dinosaurs: the ultimate guide to prehistoric life*, HarperCollins, London, 2000

INDEX

abelisaurids 28, 61
allosaurids 8, 26
amphibians 4, 7
ankylosaurids 9,
    45–6, 68
Antarctosaurus 33–5,
    38, 43
Apatosaurus 36–7
Archaeopteryx 70
armour 9, 37, 41, 43,
    44–7

battles 10–13, 31,
    32–5, 49, 56–7
beaks 4, 29, 74
birds 1, 2–3, 7, 9, 15,
    29, 40, 45, 61, 66,
    67, 70, 72–3, 74–5,
    77
bones 5, 8, 12–13,
    15–17, 18, 19, 21,
    22, 23, 24, 28, 29,
    36, 38, 40, 41, 42,
    48, 49, 51, 58–9, 61,
    63, 65–9, 74, 81
brachiosaurids 8,
    22, 42
Brontosaurus see
    Apatosaurus

camarasaurids 42
carcharodontosaurids
    26

carnivore
    see meat-eaters
Caudipteryx 72–3
ceratopsians 4, 8, 9,
    10–13, 31, 45, 47,
    48–9, 56–7
cetiosaurids 41
claws 11, 12, 27, 29,
    30, 31, 43, 34, 37, 40
coelurosaurs 25–6, 70
Confuciusornis 74
coprolites (poo stone)
    22, 23
Cretaceous Period 6,
    7, 26, 27, 30, 43, 46,
    47, 48, 49, 50, 51,
    53, 54, 57, 61, 71,
    74–5, 77–9
crocodiles viii, 1, 2, 3,
    4, 27, 45, 68–9, 77

diplodocids 38, 40, 43
dromaeosaurids
    30–1, 72, 73
dryosaurids 60

eggs 4, 5, 15, 17–18,
    23, 25, 29, 60, 63,
    64–7, 69
evolution 3, 4

fabrosaurids 60
feathers 21, 61, 70–5
fish 4, 7, 27, 63

footprints 5, 15,
    18–21, 23, 41, 47, 62
fossils 5, 12, 14–17,
    20, 21, 22, 23, 28,
    29, 47, 51, 55,
    58–60, 61, 62–3,
    64–8, 70, 74, 80–1

Giganotosaurus 25,
    26, 32–5, 61

hadrosaurids 9, 50,
    54–5, 66–7
heterodontosaurids
    50
horns 4, 9, 28, 45,
    47–8, 50, 57, 61
hypsilophodontids
    50–2, 67

iguanodonts 9, 50,
    52–4, 68

Jurassic period 6, 7,
    21, 26, 30, 41–3,
    47, 70

lizards 2, 3, 9, 26, 36,
    38, 41, 52, 65, 73, 77

Maiasaura 65
marginocephalians
    45, 47–9
meat-eaters 3, 9, 22,
    24–31, 33, 37, 41,
    51, 56–7, 66, 74, 77

Mesozoic Era 6, 7, 80
Muttaburrasaurus 53–4

nests 5, 15, 17, 23, 29, 63, 64,–7, 69, 79

ornithischians (bird-hipped) 9
ornithomimosaurs 21, 28–9
oviraptorids 29, 61, 66, 72

pachycephalosaurids 45, 49, 66
palaeontologists 12, 17, 23, 24, 29, 64–5, 81
plant-eaters 9, 22, 23, 26, 31, 33–4, 36–43, 44–9, 50–7, 67, 68, 77, 78, 79
poo 22
prey 3, 22, 29, 74
Protoceratops 4, 10–13, 31, 47–8
pterosaurs 6, 7, 77

raptors 8, 10–13, 25, 26, 29, 30–1, 61, 66, 72, 73

reptiles viii, 1, 2–3, 4, 5, 6, 7, 36, 67, 68, 70

saurischians (lizard-hipped) 9
sauropods (*see* plant-eaters)
Scipionyx 23
skeletons 8, 12, 15–17, 24, 30, 31, 37–8, 49, 51, 53, 55, 58–9, 61, 65, 66, 68–9, 74
skin 21, 37, 41, 45, 54, 55, 67, 68
skull 12, 23, 26, 46, 47, 48, 49, 63, 66
smuggling 58–63
spinosaurids 27
stegosaurids 8, 9, 45, 46–7, 62

tails 28, 34, 37, 40, 41, 43, 45, 46, 67, 69, 70, 74–5
teeth 4, 12–13, 15, 24–5, 26, 27, 28, 29, 31, 34, 37, 46, 47, 51, 52, 54, 57, 74
thecodonts 3
therizinosaurids 31, 72

theropods (*see* meat-eaters)
Thescelosaurus 23
thyreophorans 45–7
titanosaurids 33, 37–8, 43
trackways *see* footprints
Triassic period 6, 7, 25, 50
Triceratops 4, 8, 47, 48, 56–7
trilobites 7
tyrannosaurids 8, 21, 22, 24, 25, 27, 56–7, 59, 69
Tyrannosaurus rex (*T. rex*) viii, 21, 24, 26, 27, 33, 51, 56–7, 59, 61, 68–9

Unenlargia 74

Velociraptor 8, 10–13, 30, 31

wings 4, 70, 72–4